Blessings.

Peace.

Safety.

Julia A. Royston

BK
ROYSTON
Publishing

BK Royston Publishing
Jeffersonville IN
http://bkroystonpublishing.com
bkroystonpublishing@gmail.com

Cover and Layout: BK Royston Publishing

King James Version — Public Domain

The Message — Copyright © 1993, 2002,
2018 by Eugene H. Peterson

New King James Version — Scripture taken
from the New King James Version®.
Copyright © 1982 by Thomas Nelson. Used
by permission. All rights reserved.

ISBN-13: 978-1-959543-74-9

Printed in the United States of America

Dedication

I dedicate this book as a prayer to every person in this world that you walk and live in God's blessings, His Peace and His Safety.

Acknowledgments

I thank my Lord and Savior Jesus Christ for giving me another opportunity to introduce more people to you. I thank you that you have for entrusting this gift to me. Lord, let your Spirit move, guide and empower through this book to the people who will read it.

To my husband, Brian K. Royston, the love of my life for loving and cheering me on so much that I can be and do all that God has placed in me. I love you.

To my Mom, my greatest supporter and best friend. To my Dad, who is in heaven, whom I know is proud of me and always encouraged me to go for it. Thanks to all the rest of my family for their love and support.

A special thank you to Rev. and Mrs. Claude R. Royston for their love and support.

To the rest of my clients, friends and family, thank you and love you always. Let's go!

Love, Julia

Table of Contents

Blessings

Peace

Safety

Introduction

Since March of 2020, I have been signing my emails, some social media posts and text messages with "Blessings, Peace and Safety." I have been praying that people everywhere would experience God's Blessings, feel His Peace, and walk in His Safety.

In 2023, God says that it's time to put the devotional together on these three topics so that you will have some scripture to go along with His power and presence.

Enjoy!

Blessings

When people think of blessings, they only think of money, cars, houses and materials things. But the blessing of the Favor of God, Peace of Mind, Clear Vision and Pursued Purpose are Priceless.

#juliaroyston

#messagemotivator

Blessings from Heaven

Even by the God of thy father, who shall help thee; and by the Almighty, who shall bless thee with blessings of heaven above....

Genesis 49:25 (KJV)

There is an old song that says, "When praises go up, blessings come down..." I've sung that song in my life for years and truly believe it as well as have seen it happen many times. But in Genesis, Jacob gives this prophecy unto Joseph who along with his father is a direct descendant and grandson of Abraham. Just like God promised to bless Abraham and make his name great, those same blessings are pronounced upon Joseph. Joseph would be blessed with blessings from heaven up above.

God will send us, today, His adopted children by Jesus Christ Himself; blessings from heaven by way of angels, heavenly or earthly, are going to give you ideas, experiences and opportunities that will bless you now and for generations to come.

May the blessings, plural, of the Lord fall upon you now and forever.

Reflection

_____

_____

_____

_____

_____

_____

_____

_____

_____

_____

_____

_____

_____

_____

_____

_____

_____

_____

_____

_____

_____

_____

➤ · ➤ ✿ ◄ · ◄

Reflection

_____

_____

_____

_____

_____

_____

_____

_____

_____

_____

_____

_____

_____

_____

_____

_____

_____

_____

_____

_____

—⟩·⟩❁⟨·⟨—

Blessings Beyond Creation

May the blessings of your father exceed the blessings of the ancient mountains, surpass the delights of the eternal hills; May they rest on the head of Joseph, on the brow of the one consecrated among his brothers.

Genesis 49:26 (The Message)

When you fly in an airplane, there is something about being above the clouds and looking below at the earth and God's creation. The majesty of the mountains is even more pronounced in the air. While I was flying to Alaska, the mountains were so close in the air, that they looked close enough to touch although I knew I couldn't. I knew it was a mirage and not humanly possible for me while in the air but oh, what a sight to see.

Jacob in his final days and telling his sons what was to come next, pronounced such a blessing over Joseph that would exceed the blessings of the ancient mountains and all that had taken place there as well as the "delights of the eternal hills."

Clearly, blessings beyond creation. A blessing that would go beyond our imagination and wonders of even what our natural eyes could see.

Lord, you promised to do exceedingly and abundantly above all that we ask or think, but we know that you can do even more than that and give us blessings beyond the wonders of your awesome creation.

Reflection

_____

_____

_____

_____

_____

_____

_____

_____

_____

_____

_____

_____

_____

_____

_____

_____

_____

_____

_____

_____

_____

_____

—>·>❀<·<—

Reflection

_____

_____

_____

_____

_____

_____

_____

_____

_____

_____

_____

_____

_____

_____

_____

_____

_____

_____

_____

_____

_____

_____

_____

—≻·≻❀≺·≺—

Blessings of Obedience

And all these blessings shall come on thee, and
overtake thee, if thou shalt hearken unto the
voice of the Lord thy God.

Deuteronomy 28:2 (KJV)

So my parents were good at
promising to take us to get ice
cream, go on a trip or go shopping if
we worked in their business. If it
was humanly possible, my parents
would make it happen. Once we
were going to get fish sandwiches at
a famous fish place in Louisville KY.
Well, we had the money, but the
restaurant closed early. So it wasn't
my parents' fault for promising us
something but didn't deliver. They
couldn't deliver because the
restaurant was closed. We were all
disappointed, but no one blamed
our parents for promising

something and not delivering, but it wasn't humanly possible.

Now God, on the other hand, can do anything to not only have it happen or even make it happen. So He has promised that blessings would come over you and overtake you, meaning run you down, if you just obey His voice and do what He says.

Reflection

_____

_____

_____

_____

_____

_____

_____

_____

_____

_____

_____

_____

_____

_____

_____

_____

_____

_____

_____

_____

_____

_____

_____

—≳·→❀←·≲—

Reflection

_____

_____

_____

_____

_____

_____

_____

_____

_____

_____

_____

_____

_____

_____

_____

_____

_____

_____

_____

_____

_____

_____

—≻·≻❀≺·≺—

The Blessings of Goodness

For You meet him with the blessings of
goodness; You set a crown of pure gold upon
his head.

Psalm 21:3 (NKJV)

From our early years as children,
we were taught to be good, act good
and do good so that good things
would happen to us. My parents
were big on promising treats, trips
and other trinkets to get us to work
hard at school, work hard in the
business and do well in school.
Those promises were kept and
many more. I can officially say that
my sisters and I were hard workers,
but parents were loving, giving and
rewarded freely for good works.

The scripture says that even your Luke 11:13 (KJV), "If ye then, being evil, know how to give good gifts unto your children: how much more shall your heavenly Father give the Holy Spirit to them that ask him?"

In my life, I have stood on those promises. I received the Holy Spirit along with other wonderful, unmerited gifts from the heavenly Father. In Psalm 21:3, David praises God for giving him the blessings of goodness. The blessings come because God is good and not because man has been good at all.

Lord, we thank you for blessing us because, through and from your goodness and definitely not because of any goodness of our own.

Reflection

_____

_____

_____

_____

_____

_____

_____

_____

_____

_____

_____

_____

_____

_____

_____

_____

_____

_____

_____

_____

_____

_____

Reflection

_____

_____

_____

_____

_____

_____

_____

_____

_____

_____

_____

_____

_____

_____

_____

_____

_____

_____

_____

_____

_____

_____

—⇒·↘❀↙·⇐—

The Blessing from Mount Zion

As the dew of Hermon, and as the dew that descended upon the mountains of Zion: for there the Lord commanded the blessing, even life for evermore.

Psalm 133:3 (KJV)

In modern times, Mount Herman is the highest elevation controlled by Israeli territory to date. It has been historically attributed to be Mount Zion or the Mount where Jesus was transfigured.

No matter your stance in the location, historical significance or non-Israeli or Israeli point of view, in Psalm 133, David said that God commanded the blessing from the highest height and even commanded life for evermore.

God has all power both in heaven and on earth. If He commands a thing, blessing, assignment, anointing or anything, it will come to pass.

The blessing has been commanded and it is so.

Reflection

_____

_____

_____

_____

_____

_____

_____

_____

_____

_____

_____

_____

_____

_____

_____

_____

_____

_____

_____

_____

_____

—≻·≻❀≺·≺—

Reflection

_____

_____

_____

_____

_____

_____

_____

_____

_____

_____

_____

_____

_____

_____

_____

_____

_____

_____

_____

_____

_____

The Blessing on the Just

Blessings are upon the head of the just: but
violence covereth the mouth of the wicked.

Proverbs 10:6 (KJV)

"Just" is the root word for "Justice."
The right thing, not always the
popular thing, but the right thing.
The right call, decision, observation
and judgment. We need God to be
just and to administer rightful
judgment. We don't know
everything, but God knows
everything. So the scripture also
tells us, "Now the just shall live by
faith...." Hebrews 10:38 (NKJV)
Faith in what and Faith in whom?
Faith in God. God alone. That's how
the just live their daily lives to
continue to remain just. In Proverbs
10:6, if you are striving to be just,

there are blessings upon your head. Your head controls the mind, will, emotions, direction, eyes or your vision, hearing and what you say.

My prayer is God help me to be just and be worthy of the blessings that come only from You to the just.

Reflection

_____

_____

_____

_____

_____

_____

_____

_____

_____

_____

_____

_____

_____

_____

_____

_____

_____

_____

_____

_____

_____

Reflection

_____

_____

_____

_____

_____

_____

_____

_____

_____

_____

_____

_____

_____

_____

_____

_____

_____

_____

_____

_____

_____

_____

The Blessings for the Faithful

A faithful man shall abound with blessings: but he that maketh haste to be rich shall not be innocent.

Proverbs 28:20 (KJV)

As an entrepreneur, this scripture speaks volumes to me. Entrepreneurship is hard work. Sometimes even when you succeed, it comes with little appreciation or acknowledgment. Yes, I may have the financial profit from the work, but emotionally it can be draining. The scriptures tell us that the "faithful"man or person will abound in blessings. You have to keep at it, be consistent and don't quit to abound in blessings. The second part of that scripture alludes to trying to get "rich quick" is not without its ability to cut corners or possibly do some things that are immoral or not with integrity. A loss of innocence implies to me that you did something that wasn't correct, right or ethical to get rich.

Take the slow road in business, career and life. Be steady. Learn from the mistakes, shortcomings and lessons. There are blessings for the faithful.

Lord, give me the strength and courage to be faithful so that I can receive the blessings that you have in store for the faithful in this life and beyond.

Reflection

_____

_____

_____

_____

_____

_____

_____

_____

_____

_____

_____

_____

_____

_____

_____

_____

_____

_____

_____

_____

_____

_____

—≻·≻❀≺·≺—

Reflection

_____
_____
_____
_____
_____
_____
_____
_____
_____
_____
_____
_____
_____
_____
_____
_____
_____
_____
_____
_____
_____
_____

The Blessing to Make Rich

The blessing of the Lord, it maketh rich, and he addeth no sorrow with it.

Proverbs 10:22 (KJV)

It has been said — and I have said it many times — that all money is not good money. Some business opportunities and people come with more trouble than the money is worth. Yes, I said it. But the blessing of the Lord maketh rich and addeth no sorrow. It adds no regret. It adds not detriment to the brand, business, health, wellness and future of the endeavor. Now, I don't believe that the blessing of the Lord is without effort, work, prayer or direction but it shouldn't add sorrow, grief, regret, harm or deficit.

My prayer daily in my business is that God will lead me to the blessing that will make me and my family rich for the next generation and will not be a hindrance or harmful, no matter how much I need the finance, opportunity or access.

I don't want the sorrow, but I will do the work. Thank you in advance for the blessing of the Lord to make us all rich.

Reflection

_____

_____

_____

_____

_____

_____

_____

_____

_____

_____

_____

_____

_____

_____

_____

_____

_____

_____

_____

_____

_____

_____

—⟩·→✿←·⟨—

Reflection

_____
_____
_____
_____
_____
_____
_____
_____
_____
_____
_____
_____
_____
_____
_____
_____
_____
_____
_____
_____
_____
_____

Spiritual Blessings

Blessed be the God and Father of our Lord Jesus
Christ, who hath blessed us with all spiritual
blessings in heavenly places in Christ:

Ephesians 1:3 (KJV)

In the end times, which we are in
right now, people would be
deceived and deceive others. If
you're spiritually in tune at all, you
can see the deception all around. To
combat deception, you have to be as
spiritually in tune with God as
possible. Seek Him daily. Seek Him
hourly, if necessary. More
importantly, you need to ask Him
about every major decision. As I
have gotten older, spiritual
blessings are more necessary to me
than material blessings. If I have
spiritual blessings, God will lead

me, bring me to and will teach me how to get material blessings.

Lord, give us your spiritual blessings of discernment, insight, strength, courage, clear vision and heightened hearing to know your voice and walk in your ways.

Reflection

_____

_____

_____

_____

_____

_____

_____

_____

_____

_____

_____

_____

_____

_____

_____

_____

_____

_____

_____

_____

—≻·≻❀≺·≺—

Reflection

_____
_____
_____
_____
_____
_____
_____
_____
_____
_____
_____
_____
_____
_____
_____
_____
_____
_____
_____
_____
_____
_____

The Blessing on the Lamb

Saying with a loud voice, Worthy is the Lamb
that was slain to receive power, and riches, and
wisdom, and strength, and honour, and glory,
and blessing.

Revelation 5:12 (KJV)

If we serve the lamb of God who has
taken away the sins of the world,
we will enjoy the blessings of being
a part of the family of God and
worshipping the Lamb of God.

So no matter what blessings we
desire, our ultimate goal is to
worship the source, the King of
Kings and Lord of Lords and Lamb
of God who took away the sins and
now we inherit eternal life, power
from the Holy Spirit and all other
spiritual and natural blessings that

come with being a son or a daughter.

For me, God is the Worthy Lamb and Worthy to receive All power, riches, wisdom, strength, honour, glory and blessing. Now and forever. Amen.

Reflection

_____

_____

_____

_____

_____

_____

_____

_____

_____

_____

_____

_____

_____

_____

_____

_____

_____

_____

_____

_____

_____

—≫·❀·≪—

Reflection

_____

_____

_____

_____

_____

_____

_____

_____

_____

_____

_____

_____

_____

_____

_____

_____

_____

_____

_____

_____

_____

_____

_____

—≽·≻✿≺·≼—

Peace

The word peace is usually followed by the word "quiet." Think about when the house was filled with children playing, the television up loud and the dogs were barking. These words on paper even look like a lot of noise. But that God peace may be needed when you're all alone and the only noise is inside your head. No people talking. No television playing or even your phone ringing, but you still need peace. Grant peace to all who read this, in Jesus' name.

#juliaroyston

#messagemotivator

Peace Given to You

Peace I leave with you, my peace I give unto you: not as the world giveth, give I unto you. Let not your heart be troubled, neither let it be afraid.

John 14:27 (KJV)

What do you do with a gift that is given? Normally, you say, "thank you" and then keep it somewhere safe because it is precious. Jesus left peace with the disciples but then He said, "my peace" I give unto you. Wow, what a word and what a gift.

God gave His peace to the disciples and the peace He had taken Him through every trial, accusation, act of God through healings, deliverance and finally the acceptance of His ultimate assignment, the cross. This peace that Jesus gave to the disciples was clearly the peace that passeth understanding.

If we walk in the spiritual and children of God, we have that same gift. Accept the gift of Jesus' peace in your life and let that peace keep your heart from trouble and cause you to never be afraid.

Reflection

_____

_____

_____

_____

_____

_____

_____

_____

_____

_____

_____

_____

_____

_____

_____

_____

_____

_____

_____

_____

_____

—>·>❄<·<—

Reflection

_____

_____

_____

_____

_____

_____

_____

_____

_____

_____

_____

_____

_____

_____

_____

_____

_____

_____

_____

_____

_____

_____

_____

—⟩·⟩�֍⟨·⟨—

The Prince of Peace

For unto us a child is born, unto us a son is
given: and the government shall be upon his
shoulder: and his name shall be called
Wonderful, Counsellor, The mighty God, The
everlasting Father, The Prince of Peace.

Isaiah 9:6 (KJV)

The Prince of any territory has not
only responsibility but also
authority. They may not yet be the
King, but they have power and can
rule. Jesus is all divine, all human
and one with the Father. His name
was called The Prince of Peace, not
a Prince of Peace but "The" Prince
of Peace.

If anything is bothering you,
troubling you, tormenting you and
trying to take your peace, His name
has the authority to restore,

administer and bring peace to any situation.

Just say, "Jesus" and the Prince of Peace will bring the peace that you need to your heart and life.

Reflection

_____

_____

_____

_____

_____

_____

_____

_____

_____

_____

_____

_____

_____

_____

_____

_____

_____

_____

_____

_____

_____

_____

Reflection

_____

_____

_____

_____

_____

_____

_____

_____

_____

_____

_____

_____

_____

_____

_____

_____

_____

_____

_____

_____

_____

_____

Thoughts of Peace

For I know the thoughts that I think toward you,
saith the Lord, thoughts of peace, and not of
evil, to give you an expected end.

Jeremiah 29:11 (KJV)

God's power is so great that He can think things and they happen. God has you on your mind. Believe that. He has a plan for your life and has thought clearly and specifically the steps, incidences and solutions in your life. You are not an accident, but God has a plan for you and specifically customized just for you.

He not only thinks about you, but He also has thoughts of peace. He is thinking peace and not evil. He is thinking peace to come to you and your situation. His expected end will come with peace and not evil.

Evil may try to attack you but not without facing God's thoughts of peace working against the evil and working for your peace.

Reflection

_____

_____

_____

_____

_____

_____

_____

_____

_____

_____

_____

_____

_____

_____

_____

_____

_____

_____

_____

_____

_____

_____

⟶· ✤ ·⟵

Reflection

_____

_____

_____

_____

_____

_____

_____

_____

_____

_____

_____

_____

_____

_____

_____

_____

_____

_____

_____

_____

_____

_____

Seek Peace

Depart from evil, and do good; seek peace, and
pursue it.

Psalm 34:14 (KJV)

The first commandment in this
scripture is to depart from evil. It's
a plain and simple command but
sometimes for some people it is
hard to do. It seems like evil finds
them. If you leave, turn away from,
don't answer the text message,
block them from your messenger
system and phone calls, it is
sometimes easier to depart from
evil. On the other hand, there is
something else for you to do and
that is to do good. Step one is to
depart from evil. Step two is to do
good. Step three is to seek peace.
Seeking peace is a daily activity but

you should head in the direction of peace, hunt it down and chase after it if necessary. Step four is to pursue it or pursue peace. As the old movie states, "be in hot pursuit" of peace, calm, rest, quiet, stillness and away from as much non-combative, negative activity as possible.

Seek and pursue peace with all of your might. Let's go!

Reflection

_____

_____

_____

_____

_____

_____

_____

_____

_____

_____

_____

_____

_____

_____

_____

_____

_____

_____

_____

_____

_____

Reflection

_____

_____

_____

_____

_____

_____

_____

_____

_____

_____

_____

_____

_____

_____

_____

_____

_____

_____

_____

_____

_____

_____

—⟩·⟩✿⟨·⟨—

Kingdom Peace

For the kingdom of God is not meat and drink;
but righteousness, and peace, and joy in the
Holy Ghost.

Romans 14:17 (KJV)

Growing up, my faith walk was filled with rules, regulations, guidelines and obedience. I've read this scripture many times but had my foundational teachings as the guide for what the Kingdom of God really meant. I can honestly say that I stopped mostly at the righteousness part. I thought it was designed to keep me on the straight and narrow along with the rules, guidelines and regulations. But, now that I'm older and have my own relationship with God, the peace and joy in the Holy Ghost comes through more clearly. Do I allow the Holy Ghost to be my guide, lead me, guard my thoughts and ultimately my actions, of course. But now I focus even more on the Peace and Joy in the Kingdom of God. Not to water down or diminish the right living or righteousness of God in any way shape or form but know that Kingdom Peace will drive me closer to God and not away from Him.

God give us more Kingdom Peace.

Reflection

_____
_____
_____
_____
_____
_____
_____
_____
_____
_____
_____
_____
_____
_____
_____
_____
_____
_____
_____
_____
_____
_____

Reflection

_____

_____

_____

_____

_____

_____

_____

_____

_____

_____

_____

_____

_____

_____

_____

_____

_____

_____

_____

_____

_____

—⟩·⟩❀⟨·⟨—

The Peace of God

And the peace of God, which passeth all
understanding, shall keep your hearts and
minds through Christ Jesus.

Philippians 4:7 (KJV)

There are certain things in life that
happen that just can't be explained.
They fall into the category of "acts
of God," miracles, signs, wonders
and unexplainable. The Peace of
God falls into that same category
and in Philippians it is classified as
passeth all understanding. God
understands it but man can't
understand. In one scripture God
says, "My ways are not your ways
and my thoughts aren't your
thoughts." So there are some things
that God is, does and brings to pass
that you will never understand but
so glad that you have that access

and are privileged to have those experiences.

So the Peace of God which you cannot understand and goes beyond your human understanding shall keep your heart and mind only through Christ Jesus. Your believe, walk, faith and life through Christ Jesus will carry you through this life and bring you the Peace of God.

Reflection

_____

_____

_____

_____

_____

_____

_____

_____

_____

_____

_____

_____

_____

_____

_____

_____

_____

_____

_____

_____

_____

_____

Reflection

_____

_____

_____

_____

_____

_____

_____

_____

_____

_____

_____

_____

_____

_____

_____

_____

_____

_____

_____

_____

_____

—≻·≻❀≺·≺—

The Peace Look

The Lord lift up his countenance upon thee, and
give thee peace.

Numbers 6:26 (KJV)

There is the "mother look," the
"teacher look" and the look of the
Lord — which are definitely all
three different. My mother could
look at you and you'd straighten up
immediately. My parents were no
strangers to discipline, and I never
liked any of it. So when they gave
me the "look," I could get it together
really quickly.

I smile when I write this because I
never had any biological children,
but I had the "teacher look." I just
look at some students and they
would start saying, "What did I do
Mrs. Royston?" I didn't have to say

anything but just gave them the look.

No matter the circumstance, trial or test, let God lift up His countenance and give you His look that will bring you the ultimate peace.

Reflection

_____
_____
_____
_____
_____
_____
_____
_____
_____
_____
_____
_____
_____
_____
_____
_____
_____
_____
_____
_____
_____

Reflection

_____

_____

_____

_____

_____

_____

_____

_____

_____

_____

_____

_____

_____

_____

_____

_____

_____

_____

_____

_____

—>·>❀<·<—

Peace to You

And he said, Peace be to you, fear not: your God, and the God of your father, hath given you treasure in your sacks: I had your money. And he brought Simeon out unto them.

Genesis 43:23 (KJV)

In Genesis 43, Joseph has finally arrived in the palace. He has endured years of trouble from the pit, to the Potipher's house, to prison and now to the palace. He is facing his family, his brothers who started out wanting him dead and then just out of their sight, to now coming to him because of a famine and needing food for the family.

Joseph can clearly tell that they are fearful. So his words are "peace be to you." It is amazing how over time the position and situation can change in life. There are those who impose harm, misery and abuse on others who eventually will need mercy, compassion and help in the future.

The Bible clearly says, "you will reap what you sow." It is a law so be careful what you sow, because you will eventually reap. In Joseph's case, he teased and toyed with his brothers in the story, but he did not seek revenge. He had the heart of God in that he blessed them and pronounced peace be to each of them when he could have issued a punishment and refused to help.

With the help of God, the power of God and the love of God, you will be placed in the position to give the peace of God those who may not deserve it but remember that we don't deserve it either.

Reflection

_____

_____

_____

_____

_____

_____

_____

_____

_____

_____

_____

_____

_____

_____

_____

_____

_____

_____

_____

_____

_____

_____

—⟩·⟩❀⟨·⟨—

Reflection

_____

_____

_____

_____

_____

_____

_____

_____

_____

_____

_____

_____

_____

_____

_____

_____

_____

_____

_____

_____

_____

_____

Hold Your Peace

The LORD shall fight for you, and ye shall hold
your peace.

Exodus 14:14 (KJV)

At my home church, we sang a song that said, "if I hold my peace, let the Lord fight my battles; victory shall be mine."

This song is true today and always. Victory is mine if I hold my peace and let the Lord fight for me. But in Exodus, the children of Israel were told that the Lord shall fight for you. You won't need to do any fighting, just hold your peace.

I can truthfully say that there have been times that I really didn't want to hold my peace, but I did. I confess that it was hard especially since I'm not confrontational, but I learned long ago that God fights better than I ever can. Even if it takes a while, He knows just how, when and where to fight to defeat the enemy and not just get a few good licks in.

God, fight for me.

Reflection

_____

_____

_____

_____

_____

_____

_____

_____

_____

_____

_____

_____

_____

_____

_____

_____

_____

_____

_____

_____

_____

_____

—⇒·⇒❀⇐·⇐—

Reflection

_____

_____

_____

_____

_____

_____

_____

_____

_____

_____

_____

_____

_____

_____

_____

_____

_____

_____

_____

_____

_____

_____

—≻·≻❀≺·≺—

Peace Offering

And he shall offer the ram for a sacrifice
of peace offerings unto the Lord, with the
basket of unleavened bread:

Numbers 6:17 (KJV)

In the Bible, to bring peace, the
children of Israel were told to bring
a ram as a sacrifice for peace as a
peace offering unto God. A peace
offering could be a ram, sheep or
goat, depending on the status of the
family.

Even in modern times, a peace
offering could be appropriate to
bring peace into a situation or
between people. Jesus' name means
the Prince of Peace so a
characteristic of a follower of Christ
is a peace maker. What are you
willing to sacrifice to bring peace?

Are you willing to forgive, bring reconciliation or seek ways to move forward in spite of the situation? Is the argument, disagreement or matter worth keeping turmoil rather than bringing peace?

Reflection

_____

_____

_____

_____

_____

_____

_____

_____

_____

_____

_____

_____

_____

_____

_____

_____

_____

_____

_____

_____

—≻·≻✿≺·≺—

Reflection

_____

_____

_____

_____

_____

_____

_____

_____

_____

_____

_____

_____

_____

_____

_____

_____

_____

_____

_____

_____

_____

Safety

There is a song titled, "Safety," written by Dr. Oscar Williams and sung so beautifully by LeCresia Campbell. Look it up — it'll bless you. The words are beautiful, but the image of being in the arms of the most powerful, most loving, all knowing and all seeing God pierces the heart, soothes the soul and calms the spirit right down so that you can walk through any storm, situation and circumstance.

#juliaroyston

#messagemotivator

The Land in Safety

Wherefore ye shall do my statutes, and keep
my judgments, and do them; and ye shall dwell
in the land in safety.

Leviticus 25:18 (KJV)

The Children of Israel were
constantly under attack from one
enemy or another. In the Old
Testament, they were at war
fighting for or standing their
ground against an attack all of the
time. But in Leviticus, God gives
them a promise that if they kept His
statutes, judgments and were
committed to do them, they would
dwell in "the" land in safety.
Obedience would land them safely,
finally, in the land God promised
and gave them.

If we follow God, we will land, abide, dwell, inhabit, possess and prosper in safety.

Reflection

_____

_____

_____

_____

_____

_____

_____

_____

_____

_____

_____

_____

_____

_____

_____

_____

_____

_____

_____

_____

_____

_____

—≻·≻✿≺·≺—

Reflection

_____

_____

_____

_____

_____

_____

_____

_____

_____

_____

_____

_____

_____

_____

_____

_____

_____

_____

_____

_____

—⟩·⟩❀⟨·⟨—

Fruitful Land and Safety

And the land shall yield her fruit, and ye shall
eat your fill, and dwell therein in safety.

Leviticus 25:19 (KJV)

Even though you may be safe and
no one is attacking you, what if you
are not living, abiding or dwelling in
a land, city, state or space that is
fruitful? Being safe but living in lack
is still not safe. Not having your
basic needs met is a terrible state to
be in. God promised Israel that not
only would they have their basic
needs met but the land would be
fruitful, and they could eat to be
filled and not just enough to
survive.

Lord, help to live in a land that is
not only safe to live in but yields the

opportunities to be filled and not "just enough" to survive.

Keep living, moving and following God until you reach that fruitful land for you and your life.

Reflection

_____

_____

_____

_____

_____

_____

_____

_____

_____

_____

_____

_____

_____

_____

_____

_____

_____

_____

_____

_____

_____

—⟩·⟩✻⟨·⟨—

Reflection

_____

_____

_____

_____

_____

_____

_____

_____

_____

_____

_____

_____

_____

_____

_____

_____

_____

_____

_____

_____

_____

The Lord's Safety

And of Benjamin he said, The beloved of the
Lord shall dwell in safety by him; and the Lord
shall cover him all the day long, and he shall
dwell between his shoulders.

Deuteronomy 33:12 (KJV)

Have you ever been at a parade and saw a small child sitting on the shoulders of his father or grandfather? Those children have the best seat at the parade, but they also are in the safe arms of their parent, grandparent or guardian. Who is going to harm the child in those strong arms on the steady shoulders?

When Isaac was pronouncing the prophecy of the Lord upon his children, to Benjamin he said that the children of the Lord will be safe under Benjamin's watchful eye. The Lord will do the covering and protecting of Benjamin all day long, but he would also dwell between the shoulders of God. The safest in the whole wide world.

Reflection

_____

_____

_____

_____

_____

_____

_____

_____

_____

_____

_____

_____

_____

_____

_____

_____

_____

_____

_____

_____

_____

———≻·≻❀≺·≺———

Reflection

_____

_____

_____

_____

_____

_____

_____

_____

_____

_____

_____

_____

_____

_____

_____

_____

_____

_____

_____

_____

_____

_____

—⟩·→✿←·⟨—

Strong Tower and Safe

The name of the Lord is a strong tower: the righteous runneth into it, and is safe.

Proverbs 18:10 (KJV)

This scripture always reminds me of baseball. If you run and get to the base before the ball comes in the glove of the man on the opposite team manning the base, you are safe. It all depends on the ball speed, running of the baseball player and the accuracy of the throw as to whether the ball will arrive prior to you touching the base.

In Proverbs, we are told that we will always arrive safe if we run into the strong tower, which is the name of the Lord. Not our name, not the enemies' name but the name of

Lord will be that strong tower and when we run there, we will be safe.

Those outside of the strong tower of the name of the Lord, will be "out" every time.

Reflection

_____

_____

_____

_____

_____

_____

_____

_____

_____

_____

_____

_____

_____

_____

_____

_____

_____

_____

_____

_____

_____

Reflection

_____

_____

_____

_____

_____

_____

_____

_____

_____

_____

_____

_____

_____

_____

_____

_____

_____

_____

_____

_____

_____

_____

Peace. Sleep. Safety.

I will both lay me down in peace, and sleep: for thou, Lord, only makest me dwell in safety.

Psalm 4:8 (KJV)

As a child, I talked so much that my mother would say, "Julia, if you would just lay down, close your mouth and shut your eyes, you would probably go to sleep." Well, it worked. But that simple exercise only worked because I felt safe in our house.

As a matter of fact, our house was the place where a lot of people hung out. The neighborhood kids, neighbors and friends from in town and out of town, somehow always ended up at our house. Why? Because there was peace, we could easily sleep and we could dwell there in safety. No turmoil. No major disturbances besides the phone and we had two lines because of my parent's business. Other than that, peace, sleep and safety.

Reflection

_____

_____

_____

_____

_____

_____

_____

_____

_____

_____

_____

_____

_____

_____

_____

_____

_____

_____

_____

_____

_____

_____

_____

Reflection

_____

_____

_____

_____

_____

_____

_____

_____

_____

_____

_____

_____

_____

_____

_____

_____

_____

_____

_____

_____

_____

—≻·≻❀≺·≺—

Counseling for Safety

Where no counsel is, the people fall: but in the multitude of counsellors there is safety.

Proverbs 11:14 (KJV)

You are only as strong, productive and able to scale because of your mentor, coach and team. The greatest athletes from professional to collegiate level around the world still have a coach. I am a solopreneur and have done pretty well by myself, but in the past five years of business, I've realize that I can go no further without a team. You need a team to grow, you need a team to bounce ideas off of and strategize your next moves.

You can't do it alone. Even Jesus had twelve disciples. He was all God and all man but to spread the gospel, He showed us that you still need a team. Proverbs tells us that in the multitude of counsellors, advisors, coaches and mentors there is safety. You have to be careful whom you get advice from, the perspective and experience in the situation or business that you are inquiring about but you'll be safe, if you ask.

If your mental or physical health is in question, get advice from a professional who understands you and can relate to your specific situation.

You'll be better informed and make more educated decisions for you, your health, wealth, life, career and business if you just ask.

Reflection

_____

_____

_____

_____

_____

_____

_____

_____

_____

_____

_____

_____

_____

_____

_____

_____

_____

_____

_____

_____

_____

_____

—≻·≻❀≺·≺—

Reflection

_____
_____
_____
_____
_____
_____
_____
_____
_____
_____
_____
_____
_____
_____
_____
_____
_____
_____
_____
_____
_____
_____

Exalted to Safety

To set up on high those that be low; that those
which mourn may be exalted to safety.

Job 5:11 (KJV)

There are those in the world who
need help getting to where they
need to be in life. Some people need
to be protected from themselves,
the enemy and predators that just
seek to take advantage of people
based on their current position. Job
was rich, had status and could help
those that were a low estate and set
them on high. Sometimes people
don't need money but advice,
encouragement and direction. Some
people's mere personality and
expressions on their faces make
them a candidate for calamity or
attack. Those that are strong should

watch out for those that may be weak. It may only be for a season but if God brings the opportunity to you and leads you to help, look out for and help those that may not be able to help themselves.

Reach out. Have a conversation. Give direction. Make a connection so that you can lift someone's spirits and bring them to mental health, spiritual and/or physical safety so that they can live their best life.

Reflection

_____

_____

_____

_____

_____

_____

_____

_____

_____

_____

_____

_____

_____

_____

_____

_____

_____

_____

_____

_____

_____

_____

———≻·≻❀≺·≼———

Reflection

_____

_____

_____

_____

_____

_____

_____

_____

_____

_____

_____

_____

_____

_____

_____

_____

_____

_____

_____

_____

_____

_____

—≻·≻❋≺·≺—

The Call to Safety

But whoso hearkeneth unto me shall dwell
safely, and shall be quiet from fear of evil

Proverbs 1:33 (KJV)

There is something about when
your mother calls you that you
know to come quickly. When my
father called me, he used both of my
middle names and that made me
run even faster. Sometimes they
called because they had an
assignment; other times it was to
give me something, and at other
times it was for instruction. My dad
was a master teacher until
retirement and my mother taught
us every day and in church. Every
time we got in the car as a family
and the doors closed there was a
discussion of some kind. Whether

we were going someplace new, to church and don't let an issue happen, or going to a restaurant, they talked, taught and wanted us to learn for our betterment and safety.

Proverbs shows that God wants the same thing. If you listen to God, you'll be safe and dwell in a life of safety. I don't have time to tell you all of the times that God has instructed me; I was confused, but I listened and it was for my good, my betterment and more importantly for my safety. As a matter of fact, God gave me specific instructions when I was a teenager, alone and running an errand for my father. Later that same man was arrested for being a child molester. He did no harm to me because I harkened unto God and was safe.

Reflection

_____

_____

_____

_____

_____

_____

_____

_____

_____

_____

_____

_____

_____

_____

_____

_____

_____

_____

_____

_____

—❖—

Reflection

_____
_____
_____
_____
_____
_____
_____
_____
_____
_____
_____
_____
_____
_____
_____
_____
_____
_____
_____
_____
_____
_____

A Horse for War But Safety Is of the Lord

The horse is prepared against the day of battle:
but safety is of the Lord.

Proverbs 21:31 (KJV)

I love this scripture so much that I had to include it just because of the horse reference. Psalm 20:7 says, "Some trust in chariots, and some in horses: but we will remember the name of the Lord our God."

A horse was primarily available for the rich and those with money to purchase a horse. A horse was not only for breeding or as a possession but for transportation, work and battle. As someone born in horse-country, Kentucky, the home of the famous Kentucky Derby, I know up close and personal how tall, big, sturdy and sometimes dangerous a horse can be. We love to see them run races but if they were coming straight at you, you would quickly get out of the way. They are strong animals, sit the rider up high so they can be literally on top of an enemy below. It is a place of power, position and prominence.

Throughout history, a horse has helped man do many things, especially for battle. But Proverbs says, no matter what a horse can do in battle, war or work, safety and true security is of the Lord.

Reflection

_____

_____

_____

_____

_____

_____

_____

_____

_____

_____

_____

_____

_____

_____

_____

_____

_____

_____

_____

_____

_____

—⟩·⟩✻⟨·⟨—

Reflection

_____

_____

_____

_____

_____

_____

_____

_____

_____

_____

_____

_____

_____

_____

_____

_____

_____

_____

_____

_____

—⟩·→❀←·⟨—

Walk in Safety

Then shalt thou walk in thy way safely, and thy foot shall not stumble.

Proverbs 3:23 (KJV)

I confess that I have tripped and fallen going up the stairs. I wasn't watching the height of the steps or lifting up my leg high enough so I missed the step and tripped. Now, go ahead and chuckle all you want. I laugh at myself too. Some of you may or may not be physically awkward like me but trip over your words, actions and relationships which cause your life to stumble and not just your foot.

To walk in safety, you have to be careful, look down, be aware of your surroundings before you step out of a car or take another step on the sidewalk. I realize that we can't walk with our head hung down and not fall but make a habit of looking up and then look down and then move forward.

Prior to verse 23 of Proverbs 3, the scripture tells us that we can only walk in safety with God's wisdom, understanding, knowledge and discretion. When you have these things from God, by seeking Him and looking up for His guidance, then you can walk assuredly in His safety.

Reflection

_____

_____

_____

_____

_____

_____

_____

_____

_____

_____

_____

_____

_____

_____

_____

_____

_____

_____

_____

_____

Reflection

_____

_____

_____

_____

_____

_____

_____

_____

_____

_____

_____

_____

_____

_____

_____

_____

_____

_____

_____

_____

_____

—≻·≻✿≺·≼—

About the Author

Julia Royston spends her days doing what she loves: writing, publishing, speaking and coaching others to write and monetize their messages to the world.

"Helping You Get Your Message to the Masses and Turn Your Words into Wealth" is her "why" and motto. To date, Julia has written 85+ books, published 400+ books of her own and others, recorded three music CDs and coached more than 250 to turn books into businesses. She is the owner of five companies, a non-profit organization, editor of the *Book Business Bosses* Magazine as well as the host of "Live Your Best Life" heard each Sunday morning at 10:00 a.m. EST and "The Book

Business Boss Show" on Tuesdays 10:30 a.m. EST on www.envision-radio.com and a contributing author to *EnVision* Radio Magazine.

To stay connected with Julia visit www.juliaakroyston.com.

Social Media

Facebook — @juliaaroyston

IG — @juliaaroyston

LinkedIn — @juliaaroyston

TikTok — @juliaaroyston

Thank you

I trust that you enjoyed the book, *Blessings. Peace. Safety.* You can feel free to read these devotionals on a daily basis, read one per week, read one per month or whenever you need to be reassured of God's Blessings, His Peace and to dwell in His Safety.

Don't hesitate to include this book as a group Bible study. If multiple copies are needed, don't hesitate to reach out to me via email at bkroystonpublishing@gmail.com for a discount rate for multiple copies.

Julia Royston

Blessings. Peace. Safety.

Other Books By Julia Royston

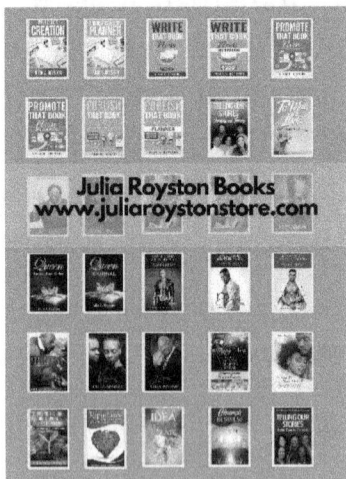

Julia Royston Books
www.juliaroystonstore.com

Julia Royston Books
www.juliaroystonstore.com
And
More to Come!

Blessings. Peace. Safety. | 131